Just Because I Am

A Child's Book of Affirmation

Lauren Murphy Payne • illustrated by Melissa Iwai

free spirit
PUBLISHING®

Library of Congress Cataloging-in-Publication Data
Payne, Lauren Murphy, 1956–
    Just because I am : a child's book of affirmation / Lauren Murphy Payne, M.S.W. ; illustrated by Melissa Iwai. — [Second edition].
        pages cm
        ISBN 978-1-63198-051-0 (hardback) — ISBN 978-1-63198-052-7 (softcover) 1. Self-perception—Juvenile literature.
2. Self-acceptance—Juvenile literature. 3. Affirmations—Juvenile literature. 4. Self-talk in children. I. Iwai, Melissa, illustrator. II. Title.
    BF697.5.S43P38 2015
    155.4'191—dc23

                                                                                            2015008014

Reading Level Grade 1; Interest Level Ages 4–8;
Fountas & Pinnell Guided Reading Level J

Edited by Pamela Espeland and Alison Behnke
Cover and interior design by Colleen Rollins

10 9 8 7 6 5 4 3 2
Printed in the United States of America
S14200416

Free Spirit Publishing Inc.
6325 Sandburg Road, Suite 100
Golden Valley, MN 55427-3674
(612) 338-2068
help4kids@freespirit.com
www.freespirit.com

To Aaron and Adam;
for Karen and the lost children;
for Scott, who always believes in me;
and for my parents, Gloria and Frederick
Murphy, without whom I would
not be who I am.

I am a person.

I am special.
I am important.

Not because of what I look like,
not because of what I have...

Just because I am.

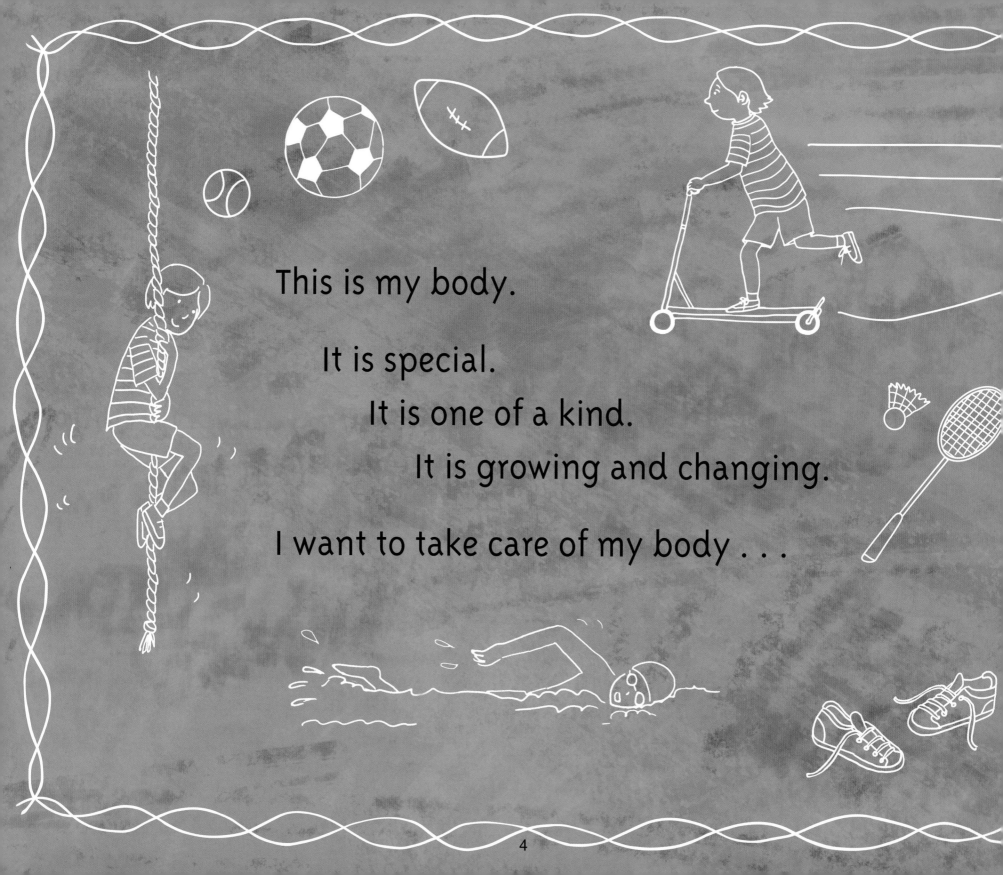

This is my body.

It is special.

It is one of a kind.

It is growing and changing.

I want to take care of my body . . .

Because it's mine.

My body talks to me.

It tells me when I'm hungry.
It tells me when I'm sleepy.
It tells me when I'm sick.

I can trust my body
to tell me what I need.

Sometimes I have strong feelings.

I feel anger.
I feel sadness.
I feel fear.
I feel love.

These feelings belong to me.

When I feel angry,
sometimes I yell.
Sometimes I cry.

Sometimes I talk to someone I love . . .

And then I feel better.

When I feel sad,

I need to cry.

I need a hug.

I need to tell someone about my sadness . . .

So I know it's okay to be sad.

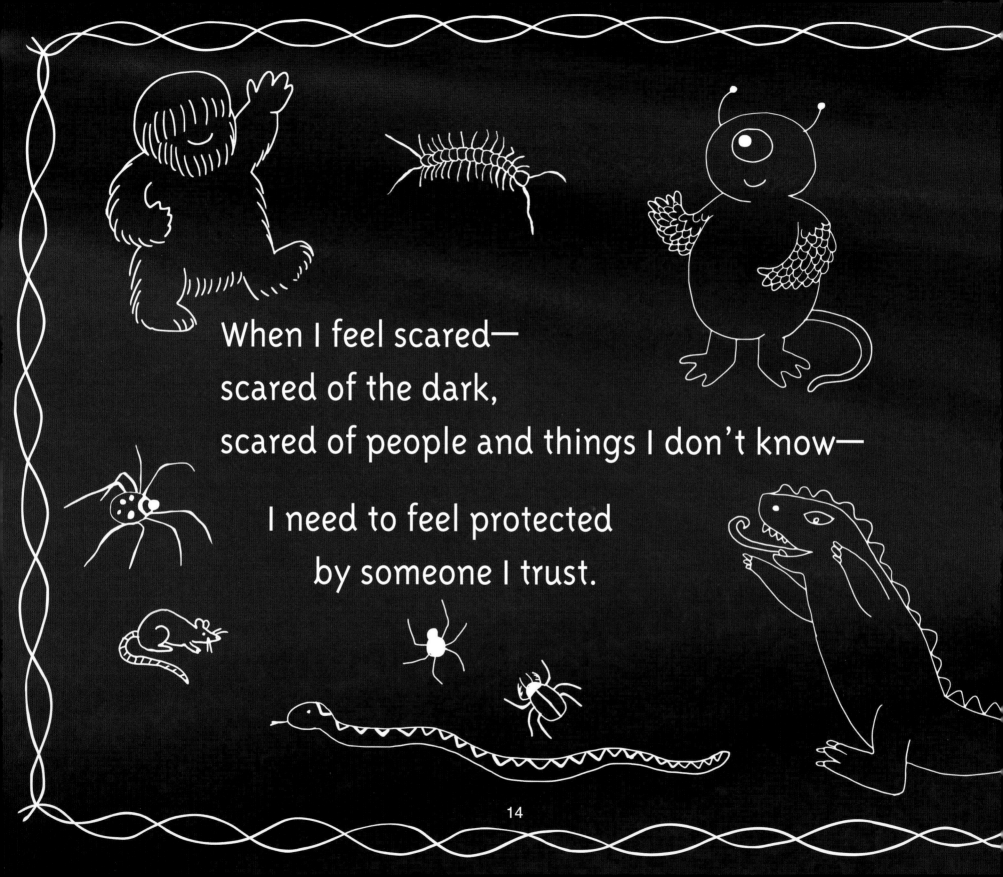

When I feel scared—
scared of the dark,
scared of people and things I don't know—

I need to feel protected
by someone I trust.

I need to feel safe.

When I feel love,

    I feel warm and snuggly.

      I feel happy and safe.

I feel important and special.

I can love myself.

I am learning and growing every day.

I learn by looking.
I learn by listening.
I learn by doing.

Sometimes I make mistakes.

That's part of learning, too.

I can make decisions.

Sometimes I say "Yes."

I say yes to playing and dancing.
I say yes to laughing and singing.
I say yes to hugging and touching . . .

When it feels right to me.

Sometimes I say "No."

I say no to danger.
I say no to hugging or touching
    that feels wrong to me.
I say no to strangers and things that hurt me . . .

I can decide.
It's up to me.

I have needs.

It's important to let people know
    what I need.
I can ask for help
    when I need it.
I can ask someone who cares about me
    to help . . .

And then I know I'm not alone.

I am myself.

I am special and unique.

My body is a part of me.

My feelings are a part of me.

My thoughts are a part of me.

My needs are a part of me.

All of these things make up a special person . . .

Me.

27

A Note to Caring Adults

Nothing is as important to a child's well-being and success as strong self-esteem. Positive self-esteem increases a child's ability to be happy, healthy, and well-adjusted. Many social and psychological problems can be traced to a lack of self-esteem. And children's feelings about themselves affect the choices they make and help shape their plans, hopes, and dreams for the future.

Just Because I Am: A Child's Book of Affirmation can be read and enjoyed with young children in many settings from preschool, school, and childcare to home, religious school, or a counseling group. The book is based on the beliefs that:

⊚ All children are inherently valuable without regard to gender, race, religion, family background, economic status, appearance, abilities, health, possessions, or any other factor.

⊚ All children have the right to feel good about themselves exactly as they are.

⊚ A child's *value* is unconditional. Nothing the child does, says, or chooses can change it.

⊚ Children can learn to accept and value their own bodies and learn to recognize what they need.

⊚ Children need to know that having needs is part of being human and that their needs are acceptable and will be met appropriately.

⊚ Children need to be taught that all of their feelings are acceptable, and that feelings are also "signals" that communicate important information.

⊚ Children need to live in an environment free from danger and fear, whether real or imagined. The need for physical and psychological safety is the most important of the basic human needs.

⊚ Children need to have a sense of power over some of the things that affect them directly and to be able to make some decisions. When we let children make decisions, we are showing them that we trust them and their abilities and in this way we let them know that they can trust themselves.

The activities and discussion starters that follow will help you build on these beliefs in a way that's fun for everyone and that makes the book's concepts come alive for children. Use the activities to encourage children to consider how they feel about themselves and to explore their individual ideas and values. The activities are designed to be flexible, so feel free to adapt them. You know your group best, so do whatever works for them. These suggestions may spark your own ideas and may serve as jumping-off points for wonderful and creative learning experiences that you invent with the children in your group. And remember to enjoy yourself! If you have fun with this book and these activities, children will have fun, too. I hope that you enjoy using *Just Because I Am* to help young children understand and appreciate how special and unique they are.

Lauren Murphy Payne, MSW, LCSW

Activities and Discussion Starters

What I Like About Me

Ask children to identify five things that they like about themselves. Say several things that you like about each child, and invite other children to add their own positive comments. Encourage children to focus on traits that are not about appearance. For example, "Carlos is good at sharing toys," or "Alexandra draws really well."

"My Body Is Mine"

Explore children's beliefs and attitudes toward their bodies. Ask questions like:

- What things does your body like to do?
- What are things that your body does well?
- What things are hard for your body to do?
- When does your body feel healthy and happy?
- What things can you do to treat your body well and take good care of it?
- What does your body tell you? What can you learn by listening to your body?

Have children complete the sentence: "I like the way my body feels when _____."

Learning and Talking About Feelings

Talk with children about the wide range of feelings they might experience—even within a single day. Ask questions like:

- What are some of the strong feelings that you have?
- Where do you feel your feelings in your body?
- Who can you talk with about your strong feelings?
- How can you tell the difference between your feelings? For example, does anger feel the same as fear? How do they feel similar? How do they feel different?
- What are some words you can use to name your feelings?

Reinforce children's right to have and feel their feelings. Acknowledge and validate their ideas, problems, fears, and concerns.

Teaching About Body Safety and Secrets

When teaching children about their bodies and feelings, it's important to talk with them about keeping their bodies safe. It's also important to discuss secrets. Children need to know the difference between a surprise (such as a birthday party) and a secret that feels bad (such as a touch that makes a child feel uncomfortable). Let children know that they *never* have to keep secrets (especially those that feel bad to them), and that there is nothing that they can't talk about with a trusted adult—even if someone else (including another adult) has told them they will get in trouble or that something really bad will happen if they tell.

If a child does disclose something to you, or if you suspect that a child is being abused, follow the established protocols of your school and district immediately if you are working in a school. You can also contact your local social service department or child welfare department, or obtain information about what to do and how to report child abuse from your local police department or district attorney's office. *Never* attempt to interview a child yourself. Instead, leave that to professionals who have been specially trained to deal with this sensitive issue.

Living Statues

Begin by asking children to think of times when they felt nervous, scared, or worried. Invite them to share some of their experiences if they feel comfortable doing so. Next, ask them to pretend that they are statues and to pose in ways that show how they feel when they are afraid or anxious. While children are posing, ask them questions such as:

◎ When does your statue feel scared or nervous?

◎ How does your statue show that it feels afraid?

◎ Where in its body does your statue feel scared or worried feelings?

◎ What might help your statue feel better?

After everyone has had a chance to pose and to talk about what they feel, ask children to change their statues into poses that feel brave and powerful. Ask follow-up questions about this different stance and feeling. For example:

◎ How do you feel when you stand in this pose?

◎ What are ways your body can help you feel strong and confident?

◎ When do you feel brave? What are some ways you can be brave even when you feel nervous about a situation?

. . . .

Asking for Help

Emphasize to children that asking for help when they need it is a good choice, and grown-ups can help them cope with challenging situations and feelings. Invite children to think about adults they could ask for help, such as teachers, parents, grandparents, other family members, or counselors (at school or elsewhere).

. . . .

Who Can Help?

After talking with children about asking for help when they need it, build on this idea through role playing. Present children with examples of problems people might have that they need help with, and invite them to add their own ideas. Examples could include:

◎ Geoffrey is having trouble putting together a puzzle.

◎ Mei Lin and her friend can't agree on who gets to play with the building blocks first.

◎ Wallace wants to look at one of his favorite books, but it's on a shelf too high for him to reach.

◎ Maria has a stomachache.

Next, invite children to brainstorm and act out ways to ask for help in these scenarios. Talk about how they can practice asking for help and use these ideas if and when similar situations arise in their own lives. If desired, rather than using direct role play, children can use dolls, puppets, or action figures to act out scenes.

Listening to Your Body and Your Feelings

Give each child a blank copy of a body outline, or have each child lie down on a large piece of paper so that you can trace his or her outline. Tell children that they can draw pictures on their body outlines to show where they feel their feelings in their bodies. Ask them to use different colors to identify different feelings (such as sadness, anger, happiness, love, or fear). If they like, children can draw images that represent their feelings, or they can simply create colored areas, scribbles, or patterns.

Ask questions like:

◎ When you feel angry, where do you feel it in your body?

◎ What happens in your body when you feel sad?

◎ What color shows how your stomach feels when you are worried?

Learning from Mistakes

It's helpful for children to know and understand that learning takes many forms, and learning doesn't happen only in school. We all can learn every day, during each moment of our lives. Talk with children about the learning that can come from "making mistakes." Help them recognize that everyone makes mistakes—no matter who they are, how old they are, or how smart they are. Talk with children about the fact that some of the most important learning we do comes from the mistakes we make. Invite them to tell about some of the mistakes they have made. Ask questions like:

◎ How did you feel when that happened?

◎ What did you learn from that?

◎ What could you do differently next time?

Be sure to stress the positive nature of the learning experience rather than focus on the mistake itself. Affirm the value of this learning by saying things like:

◎ You really learned a lot from that.

◎ It's a really good thing that you learned that!

◎ That's an important thing to learn.

Talking About Love

Help children identify some of the things that help them feel loved. Ask questions like:

◎ What does love feel like to you?

◎ How do you know when you are loved?

◎ Do you love yourself? How do you know?

◎ What do you do to show that you love yourself?

◎ How do you show love for others?

Invite children to share examples of loving things from their lives.

Lists About Feelings and Taking Care of Yourself

Use the following lists as starting points for conversations about feelings, self-esteem, and how children can take good care of themselves and their needs. Read each list aloud to children. You may also display images to represent list items and help young children understand them. You'll find suggestions for additional activities following each list.

15 Ways to Say No

- "NO."
- "Stop it."
- "I don't like that."
- "I feel uncomfortable."
- "No, thank you."
- "I don't want to play like that."
- "That hurts my feelings."
- "I don't want to."
- "No way!"
- "I mean it."
- "I feel angry about that."
- "That's not my style!"
- "I'm going to do something else right now."
- "I really don't want to do that."
- "That doesn't feel good."

Give children examples of situations where they might need to use these statements or others like them. Help children identify words they could say that would fit each situation. For example:

- Abby and Juanita are playing with a ball. Abby takes the ball and starts throwing it at Juanita. How can Juanita respond?
- If Josef and Lucinda are drawing together and Lucinda tells Josef that his ideas are dumb, how can Josef reply?
- Jessica is trying to convince Antoine to do something dangerous. What can Antoine say to Jessica?

Caleb and Peter are playing together on the playground. Caleb sees a child they don't know and tells Peter they should go tease her. What can Peter say?

10 Ways to Say Yes

- "Yes, please."
- "That sounds fun!"
- "I'd like that."
- "Okay!"
- "I'm happy about that."
- "That's a great idea."
- "Yeah, thanks!"
- "Awesome!"
- With a smile and a nod.
- With a thumbs-up.

Talk with children about times when they might say yes and could use statements from the list. Invite children to explain when and why they might say *yes*. What are situations where they might not be sure whether to say *yes* or *no*? How can they decide what feels right?

As an extension to the conversation, provide children with a variety of photos and illustrations from magazines or other sources.

(Older children may choose and cut out pictures themselves.) Explain that children can pick out pictures showing things they like—things they would say *yes* to. Give each child paper and glue and help them make collages from their pictures. Children can also draw their own pictures on their collages. If you prefer, this can be a group activity, with everyone contributing to one large collage.

15 Ways to Take Care of Yourself

- Rest when you're tired.
- Cry when you feel sad.
- Learn when to say NO.
- Be honest about your feelings and what you need.
- Ask for help when you need it.
- Eat healthful food.
- Exercise. Move your body around!
- Talk about how you're feeling with someone you love.
- Play with friends, or make a new friend.
- Spend time outdoors.
- Color, paint a picture, sing a song, or do a dance.
- Celebrate being you! Say nice things to yourself.
- Do something nice for someone else.
- Learn about something new.
- Play make-believe.

Talk with children about ways they take care of themselves. Give them paper and crayons or colored pencils and ask them to draw pictures of themselves doing something to take care of themselves. Ask them to share their pictures with the group and talk about what they drew and why.

15 Healthy Ways to Deal with Sadness

- Cry.
- Talk about your sadness with someone you trust.
- If there is something you need, ask for it.
- Wrap yourself in a blanket.
- Listen to music.
- Draw a picture.
- Watch a funny show or movie.
- Look at your favorite book.
- Play with your friends.
- Remember that it's okay to feel sad sometimes.
- Find some quiet time.
- Take a deep breath.
- Take a walk.
- Get a hug.
- Pet an animal.

Talk with children about times when they feel sad. Let them choose solutions from the list (or suggest other ideas) and discuss with them how those ideas would help them with their sadness. Ask children to think in detail about these ideas. For example, "What is a funny show or movie that always makes you laugh?" or "Who are some friends you could play with when you are sad? How could they help you feel better?" or "Who would you like to get a hug from when you are feeling sad?"

About the Author

Lauren Murphy Payne, MSW, LCSW, is a psychotherapist in private practice with 30 years of experience. She specializes in the treatment of adult survivors of childhood sexual abuse, relationship issues, anxiety, depression, and eating disorders. Lauren has been a speaker at local, regional, and national conferences. She is the author and presenter of two video series: *Making Anger Work for You* and *Anger as a Fear Driven Emotion*. She is the mother of two adult children and lives in Wisconsin with her husband.

About the Illustrator

Melissa Iwai received her BFA in illustration from Art Center College of Design in Pasadena, California. She lives in Brooklyn, New York, and has illustrated many picture books, which can be seen at www.melissaiwai.com.

Other Great Books from Free Spirit

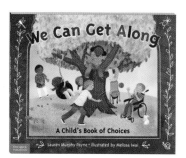

We Can Get Along
A Child's Book of Choices
by Lauren Murphy Payne, illustrated by Melissa Iwai
36 pp., color illust., HC & PB, 11¼" x 9¼".
Ages 4–8.

Feel Confident!
A book about self-esteem
by Cheri J. Meiners, M.Ed., illustrated by Elizabeth Allen
40 pp., color illust., HC & PB, 11¼" x 9¼".
Ages 4–8.

I Like Being Me
Poems about kindness, friendship, and making good choices
by Judy Lalli, M.S.
64 pp., B&W photos, color illust., PB, 8" x 8".
Ages 4–8.

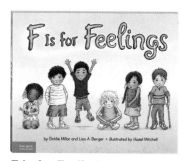

F Is for Feelings
by Goldie Millar and Lisa Berger, illustrated by Hazel Mitchell
40 pp., color illust., HC & PB, 11¼" x 9¼".
Ages 3–8.